eflete

Earl of Littlehampton K. G.

The Littlehampton Bequest

The
Littlehampton
Bequest

OSBERT LANCASTER

DRAYNFLETE ABBEY

Foreword by
ROY STRONG

Gambit
Incorporated
Boston
1974

OSBERT LANCASTER'S OTHER WORKS

PROGRESS AT PELVIS BAY

PILLAR TO POST

HOMES SWEET HOMES

HERE OF ALL PLACES

ALL DONE FROM MEMORY (*autobiography*)

WITH AN EYE TO THE FUTURE (*autobiography*)

CLASSICAL LANDSCAPE WITH FIGURES

SAILING TO BYZANTIUM

THE SARACEN'S HEAD

DRAYNEFLETE REVEALED

FAÇADES AND FACES

Pocket Cartoons

SIGNS OF THE TIMES 1939–1961

FASTEN YOUR SAFETY BELTS

TEMPORARY DIVERSIONS

MEANINGFUL CONFRONTATIONS

STUDIES FROM THE LIFE

PRIVATE VIEWS

THEATRE IN THE FLAT

First American printing
Copyright © 1973, 1974 by Osbert Lancaster
All rights reserved including the right to reproduce
this book or parts thereof in any form
Library of Congress Catalog Card Number: 74–84419
International Standard Book Number: 0–87645–087–7
Printed in the United States of America
Published in Great Britain
by John Murray (Publishers) Ltd.

CONTENTS

NOTES ON ADDITIONAL
ILLUSTRATIONS

JACKET. Until very recently this splendid picture, a late work of Peter Tillemans, hung in the harness-room at Drayneflete Abbey, where it had become so begrimed that the figures were no longer readily identifiable. Indeed, in the old hand-list, it is catalogued as *Queen Victoria and the Prince Consort at the Aldershot Review*. When, on the instructions of the present Countess, it was taken down and carefully cleaned, it was discovered to be a portrait group of the 1st Earl, his wife and elder son in the livery of the Drayneflete Hunt outside the great gates of the Park, of which each pier bears the proud crest of the Courantsdairs, a Saracen's Head proper, with, in the background, Hawksmoor's triumphal column, erected to commemorate the Glorious Revolution of 1688.

TITLE-PAGE. Drayneflete Abbey, from a 17th-century woodcut.

FRONT ENDPAPER. Drayneflete Abbey from Colin Campbell's *Vitruvius Britannicus*, 1715–1771.

BACK ENDPAPER. Drayneflete Abbey from an engraving in *The Beauties of England and Wales*, 1815.

FOR VIOLET AND TONY

FOREWORD

Few collections representative of the whole history of English portraiture can rival that of the Littlehamptons of Drayneflete. Van Dyck and Lely, Reynolds and Gainsborough, Romney and Lawrence, Burne-Jones and Millais, Sargent and Hockney are but a few of the artists whose work adds lustre to a collection notable above all for its richness in the likenesses of those who have shaped this island's history. The Littlehampton Bequest therefore rightly constitutes, in one magnificent gesture, the most significant addition to the National Portrait Gallery's holdings since the last war. Thanks to the enthusiastic persistence of the Countess of Little-hampton in her negotiations with Her Majesty's Government (and much to the relief of the Editor of the letters page of *The Times*) the Littlehampton Collection has passed intact to the nation. It is of course greatly to be lamented that space will not as yet permit even a temporary display of these historic treasures. In the meantime, however, a careful programme of cleaning and conservation is being carried out under the expert direction of Dr. Ernest Swaboff, whose restoration of the *Drayneflete Madonna*, now in the National Gallery, already stands as a monument to his ingenuity in re-covering what had for long acted as a section of the chancel floor in the Chapel at Drayneflete. At the same time research into the history of the family and the detailed documentation of each portrait is being undertaken by Miss Provenance of our curatorial staff.

The Drayneflete Collection is an historic one long referred to in the annals of art in this country. Indeed the earliest reference to the collection occurs in the Notebooks of that pioneer of the history of the arts in England, the antiquary George Vertue. On February 26th 1720 Vertue visited the collection and described it as follows: 'Drayneflete – seat of the Earl of Littlehampton – in the gallery. Cleopatra by Cranach, Sir Nicholas de Littlehampton by Gerrat and several other olde pictures on bord – in the hall – Lord Drayneflete on horseback by Van Dyck. fine.' Thereafter some reference to the Drayneflete portraits figures in every description of the great houses of this country from the peregrinations of Pennant and Dr. Syntax to the charming account of the house in *The Beauties of England and Wales* (1815) and Dr. Waagen's critical appraisal in the 1854 edition of his *The Treasures of Great Britain and Ireland*. Not long after the earliest scholarly catalogue of the collection was compiled by Lady Ethel Littlehampton. This was printed in a limited edition of one hundred copies with the finest portraits reproduced in sepia photogravure. With this the serious academic study of the Littlehampton Collection may be said to begin. My predecessor, Sir Lionel Cust, soon after contributed an article to *The Burlington Magazine* reconstructing the *œuvre* of an early English portrait-painter he called the 'Drayneflete Master', since unfortunately proved to be the work of no less than three separate painters, French, Italian and Dutch. Thenceforward items in the collections have been the subject of lively interchange in the world of learning.

It remains for me to say how indebted the Trustees are to Mr. Osbert Lancaster for recording for us the results of his researches into the Littlehampton family and their portraits.

National Portrait Gallery   ROY STRONG

INTRODUCTION

When it was suggested to me by Dr. Strong that I should provide some biographical notes for this sumptuous catalogue of a magnificent bequest, I readily and delightedly agreed. Although not a professional historian, a longstanding friendship with the family and a close familiarity with the house and its contents encouraged me to believe that I could overcome the disadvantages imposed by an amateur status. In so far as I may be thought to have done so, it is largely due to the limitless encouragement, unbounded enthusiasm and extraordinary range of information of the present Countess. Indeed had I not had Lady Littlehampton constantly by my side, while my task might have been concluded far sooner, it would have been infinitely less enjoyable. To her and the Earl I owe a debt of gratitude which the present volume can only inadequately discharge.

To those of my readers who may chance to be acquainted with an earlier work, dealing with the history and antiquities of Drayneflete,* some apology, I feel, is due for certain discrepancies which they may detect between the two texts. Much additional research has been carried out in the Littlehampton Archives in the last twenty years and, moreover, I must confess that in the former work I relied a little too confidently on the authority of a distinguished local historian, the late Miss Dracula Parsley-ffigett, herself a member of an ancient and distinguished county family, who was certainly enthusiastic but neither professionally trained nor invariably impartial. Thus her claim that her niece Consuelo was ever married to, let alone divorced from, the present Earl is quite without foundation. The cousins were certainly good friends and there were at one time rumours of an engagement but no banns were ever called. Less important but perhaps more aggravating is her constant carelessness about dates and generations, thus the 3rd Earl is regularly referred to as the 2nd and the 4th as the 5th, etc. Equally exasperating is her phonetic spelling of the family name 'Courantsdair' (pronounced Currander) – an error which arose, presumably, from dictation. Far less forgivable, however, is the quite unjustified assertion that the 6th Earl sold Drayneflete for a lunatic asylum and public park in 1887. The facts are as follows. Spending all his time on his Scottish

*Drayneflete Revealed (John Murray, 1949).

estates and never coming South the 6th Earl threw open the park to the public on Sundays and holidays when the family were not in residence. Some years later after the break-up of his first marriage, the 7th Earl leased the North Wing to a Home of Rest for the Mentally Underprivileged of Gentle Birth of which his sister, the Lady Ethel, remained the enthusiastic patron until, in 1946, it came under the administration of the Ministry of Health.

Readers should, therefore, bear in mind that invaluable as the former volume may be for those interested in the local history of Drayneflete or the genealogy of the Parsley-ffigetts, as a chronological account of the Earldom of Littlehampton it is less than reliable. The author hereby apologizes for his errors of twenty years past and trusts that the present biographical notes will have served finally to put the record straight.

O.L.

The Littlehampton Bequest

WHEN the 3rd and last Earl of Littlehampton, of the first creation, lost his head on Tower Hill, having unfortunately backed the wrong Rose, the sole remaining representative of this illustrious family was his infant daughter, Agnes. As all her father's vast estates were forfeit to the Crown, his treasure dispersed and the great Keep of Courantsdair dismantled, her lot was miserable indeed. The poor waif was finally taken by her devoted nurse to a small priory at Sloppingham in Norfolk, of which a distant cousin on her mother's side was Prioress, where it seemed likely that, undowered as she was, she would end her days. However, she grew into a lively and attractive child and at High Mass one Lammastide she caught the eye of a rich merchant from Lynn, who had some farms in the neighbourhood, and by Candlemas they were man and wife.

Nicholas Wouldbegood was one of the most successful and important of 15th-century tycoons, with a fine house in Lynn from the watch-tower of which he could keep an eye on his merchantmen, anchored in the Ouse, and with counting-houses in London and Bruges. With the accession of Edward IV, whose fondness for the company of successful businessmen, and their wives, was as marked as that of his seventh namesake four hundred years later, his influence was much increased and in 1480 he was granted a Royal Letters Patent to adopt the name and arms of de Courantsdair.

Perhaps as a result of the penury she had known as a child, it is recorded that Dame Agnes soon developed a head for business no whit inferior to her husband's and used regularly to accompany him on his travels both to London, where she was soon welcome in Court Circles, and to Bruges, where it seems likely that this exquisite likeness, the right panel of a triptych of which the centrepiece is now in the Metropolitan, was painted.

About the identity of the artist there has been much dispute; Friedlander at first assigned it to one of the Van Eycks, but Dvořák detected in the painting of the background the unmistakable hand of Dirk Bouts. At the moment it would seem wise to accept the current attribution to the Master of the Foolish Virgins, so called after his masterpiece formerly in a church in Hertogenbosch, long since vanished, by whom no other work whatever is known to exist. Of the opposite panel, which presumably exhibited a portrait of Master Wouldbegood, no trace, alas, has ever been found.

DAME AGNES DE COURANTSDAIR
Master of the Foolish Virgins [?]

THE EXACT DATE of Wouldbegood-Courantsdair's death has not been established but his widow, who was many years his junior, was still flourishing in the early years of Henry VIII's reign. Their eldest son, Benjamin, who inherited both his father's acumen and his mother's political adroitness, soon attracted the notice of the young sovereign. To his wide knowledge of foreign parts and command of languages was added, after the fall of Wolsey, a zealous enthusiasm for the Reformed Faith. With these advantages his career at Court, in days when there existed no professional diplomatic service, advanced rapidly, and was suitably rewarded. In 1548 he was made a Clerk to the Privy and was able to acquire, for a very reasonable sum, all the lands and buildings of Drayneflete Abbey, and the following year he was knighted.

Of his first wife we know little. She was the daughter of an Alderman of the City of London and a Past Master of the Drumstretchers' Company and did not, reportedly, come to him empty-handed. Their marriage although apparently happy was comparatively brief as she died of the plague after presenting him with two daughters and a son, born in successive years.

In difficult times Sir Benjamin's sound sense and unswerving devotion to the monarch's interests enabled him to avoid every pitfall. In King Edward's reign he enjoyed the position of an elder statesman and received the Priory of Sloppingham, the scene of his parents' romance, together with eleven farms and a water-mill as a testimony of his sovereign's affection. With the accession of Queen Mary, his business interests caused him to spend much time abroad and it seems likely that he died while on a visit to his second wife's relations in the Palatinate.

He left a very considerable fortune to his sons but did not neglect the poor and needy for whom he provided on a generous scale. Today his benevolence is still remembered annually on the first Thursday after Epiphany with the distribution in the churchyard of St. Ursula-inside-the-Wardrobe, of 'Old Ben's Bounty', as it is commonly called, a blood-pudding, a bundle of faggots and two groats apiece, to twelve indigent but sober old men residing in the parish.

18

BENJAMIN DE COURANTSDAIR
School of Holbein

MANY would claim that this exquisite masterpiece is the gem of the whole Bequest; none could dispute that it possesses the most romantic history.

At a time when King Henry VIII was hoping to establish closer relations with the Protestant Princes of Germany, Sir Benjamin found himself on a secret mission to the Court of the Elector Maurice of Saxony. One day this affable ruler took the Englishman on a visit to the studio of his friend and protégé, Lucas Cranach. Here the visitor was immediately struck dumb by the beauty of a panel of Cleopatra by the banks of the Nile about to drain the fatal draught in which she had previously dissolved a pearl, which he at once acquired and took back to his lodgings. The more he gazed on his purchase the more determined he became to make the acquaintance of the fair original. Luckily this did not prove difficult as Cleopatra, under the name Gertrud von der Leberkranz, was well known in Court Circles. She was the daughter of a celebrated Captain of *landsknecht*, Gottfried von der Leberkranz, and a 'liberated' nun (whether her birth took place before or after the liberation is not recorded), and received her visitor with her habitual courtesy and charm. Albeit she was now a few years older than she appeared in the painting, her admirer's expectations were abundantly fulfilled and he straightway offered her his hand which was immediately accepted. (This is the only recorded instance of Sir Benjamin ever having acted on impulse.) A few days later, after a brief ceremony in the Court Chapel, the King's emissary returned to his native country with his painting and his bride. Of the latter's subsequent history we know little. She presented her husband with a son soon after the homecoming and both as a wife and widow occupied a much respected position in the City's Lutheran community. She died in 1575 and was buried in the Dutch Church at Austin Friars where her beautiful tomb survived the Great Fire, only to fall victim to the ferocity of her fellow countrymen in 1941.

For many years this wonderful picture was completely lost sight of, until the present Countess located it in the servants' hall, to which it had been relegated by the 5th Countess, a woman of strong principles, after she had commissioned her friend, Mr. Frith, R.A., to provide her predecessor with a thick flannel nightdress, now happily removed.

'CLEOPATRA'
Lucas Cranach the Elder

W HILE inheriting to the full his father's business enthusiasm, Sir Nicholas's ambitions became, with time,
increasingly dynastic. Pulling down what remained of
Drayneflete Abbey he built himself a splendid many-windowed
manor-house in the contemporary style on the site. He married,
early in Queen Elizabeth's reign, the younger daughter of the 9th
Baron Venison, generally referred to in Court Circles as 'the Haunch'.
Her family was known to be impoverished, and suspected of being
recusant, but for the bridegroom her lack of dowry and, it must
ungallantly be added, looks, were more than compensated for by the
distinction and number of her quarterings, and the marriage was a
singularly happy one.

However, while establishing himself ever more firmly in the
ranks of the landed gentry Sir Nicholas did not neglect his commercial
interests which tended, however, to become more exclusively financial
in character as time went on. Despite the fact that in Gheeraerts's
portrait his finger is apparently resting on the Caribbean, there is
no evidence that he himself ever went further west than Hampton
Court. Nevertheless his was an important and glorious role in the
great expansionist movement of this Golden Age; few syndicates of
which he was a member ever produced an unfavourable balance
sheet and on his death, at the turn of the century, he left his elder
son, Christopher, vast estates and an immense fortune in bullion.

On the magnificent Courantsdair tomb, formerly in St. Ursula-
inside-the-Wardrobe,* the splendid effigies of himself and wife are
accompanied by the kneeling figures of their nine children only
three of whom reached riper years, and surmounted by innumerable
blazons. Unfortunately the artist responsible for Lady de Courantsdair's
portrait here reproduced remains unknown, but his work is distinguished from that of the majority of his contemporaries by
a certain charming naturalism which finds its happiest expression in
the treatment of the infant in arms.

*Transferred to the Chapel of Drayneflete Abbey after the demolition of St.
Ursula's in 1968.

LADY DE COURANTSDAIR
Artist unknown

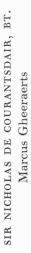

SIR NICHOLAS DE COURANTSDAIR, BT.
Marcus Gheeraerts

OF Sir Benjamin's son by his second marriage we unfortunately know little. He would seem not to have had much in common with his half-brother, spending more time at Court than in the counting-house where he soon gained a reputation as a skilled poetaster and a dexterous performer in the pavane. As a young man he spent some years in the household of the Earl of Southampton and there are those who maintain, but Dr. Rowse is not among them, that he was the original Dark Lady of the Sonnets.

He was known, at least on one occasion, to have trailed a pike in the Low Countries when there were those among his companions who loudly proclaimed that in his case 'trailed' was the operative word.

With the accession of James I his social success markedly increased and no masque was regarded as worth the watching in which he did not have a prominent role, but with the onset of middle age he rapidly put on weight and his sovereign's anxiety to have him always about his person became less acute. At the same time his half-brother's reluctance to pay the debts which his personal extravagance incurred became more marked, and soon the Court revels knew him no more. He ended his days in almost total obscurity, living on the charity of his nephew. He never married.

AUBREY DE COURANTSDAIR
Nicholas Hilliard

AMONG the many carefree young gallants at the Court of King Charles I few cut so dashing a figure as Christopher de Courantsdair. High-spirited, handsome and enormously wealthy, he was equally popular with both sexes and his devotion to the House of Stuart was absolute. When the war broke out he immediately placed himself and his fortune at the disposition of his sovereign and none among the Cavaliers surpassed him in gallantry, although, it must be admitted that few displayed such tactical incompetence.

With the final defeat of the Royal cause he accompanied the Heir Apparent into exile, loyally remaining at his side until the Restoration. It is pleasant to record that his devotion did not go unrewarded; not only were his estates restored to him, but on his marriage to an old friend of the King he was created Viscount Drayneflete and made Master of the Ordnance, and he continued high in the Royal favour until the very end of the reign. It was, perhaps, the jealousy such marked favour aroused which earned him the title of 'the Wicked Lord', for it is hard to see that he exceeded in iniquity the majority of his contemporaries. While it is just possible that the tale of his seduction of the eleven-year-old daughter of the Bishop of Barnstaple in her father's vestry may have some foundation in fact, there would seem little to justify the frequent charges of sodomy. On the only occasion that he appeared before a magistrate, on a charge of indecent exposure in the Mall – 'flashing his Littlehampton' as the Court wits put it – the principal witness was discovered to be a notorious Anabaptist and the case was dismissed. He died in 1675 and is buried in a splendid tomb by the celebrated Rysbrack in the Littlehampton Chapel in Drayneflete Church.

THE VISCOUNT DRAYNEFLETE
Van Dyck

WHEN Viscount Drayneflete went into exile with his sovereign he was accompanied by his younger brother Guy. A studious and, compared to his brother, unglamorous youth, he soon abandoned the Royal entourage in the Low Countries and made his way to Rome, where he not only reverted to the faith of his mother's family, but took Orders. Great was the rejoicing in Vatican circles at the return to the fold of so prominent a lost sheep, and he was soon comfortably installed in the household of Cardinal Azzolino where, it is said, he played an important part in the conversion of Queen Christina.

Amiable and hospitable, his apartments in the Palazzo Condotti became in time a place of pilgrimage for his countrymen passing through Italy, among them John Evelyn, who viewed his extremely comfortable way of life, and in particular 'a little sloe-eyed serving wench', with Protestant disapproval. While conscientious in fulfilling all his ecclesiastical duties he did not abandon those sporting diversions characteristic of an English gentleman and was reckoned the best shot in the Curia; nor did he neglect to cultivate scholarly pursuits, publishing a large folio volume, *De Gustibus Romanorum*, in which he gives no less than thirty-two different recipes for stuffing a partridge.

When in 1769 the 3rd Earl of Littlehampton was in Rome on the Grand Tour he had the curiosity to visit his great-great-uncle's lodgings which he found to be carefully preserved, in the condition in which he left them at the time of his death, by a withered crone of immense age (could this have been John Evelyn's 'sloe-eyed serving wench'?) from whom, with some difficulty, he managed to acquire this splendid bust.

MONSIGNOR DE COURANTSDAIR
Bernini (from a contemporary engraving)

LOUISE, the young wife of the elderly Baron de Stellenbosch who did so much to render life tolerable for King Charles II during his exile, was said by general report to have come from an armigerous Walloon family residing in Antwerp, but there were those who declared her to be the natural daughter of the Cardinal-Archbishop of Utrecht. Whatever her origins all were agreed on her beauty and her sympathetic nature. She first met the exiled monarch under her husband's roof and a rewarding and comparatively long-standing relationship soon developed. When the King came into his own again she accompanied him to London, the Baron having tactfully died a month or two earlier, but it is sad to have to relate that their delightful intimacy did not long survive the sea-change. Yet, despite new involvements, the monarch remained ever mindful of all her kindness and saw to it that she was firmly established in a state suitable to her rank, and upon her marriage to his old friend, Sir Christopher de Courantsdair, the bridegroom was immediately raised to the peerage and the bride received not only a number of very good livings but also a monopoly on the import of Dutch gin.

At Court where she immediately secured, and long retained, a prominent position, she commanded universal admiration and her charms were celebrated in the verses of Rochester and the paintings of Lely. 'To the playhouse', writes Pepys, 'where I was mightily pleased to find myself in company with my lady Drayneflete.' Towards the end of her life she became notably pious and developed an extraordinary enthusiasm for sermons, the longer the better, although it was generally agreed that her pew in the Chapel Royal was always well supplied with that commodity of which she enjoyed the monopoly.

THE VISCOUNTESS DRAYNEFLETE
IN THE CHARACTER OF ARTEMIS
Sir Peter Lely

AUGUSTUS DE COURANTSDAIR succeeded his father, the 1st Viscount Drayneflete, while still a child. Coming of a family devoted to the Stuarts and with an uncle at the Vatican, it might have been thought that he had a great future at Court, but his natural sagacity rendered him mistrustful of King James's chances, and in fact few of the nobility gave so enthusiastic a welcome to Dutch William. His foresight was soon rewarded and after the Battle of the Boyne, at which he arrived, a little late, at the head of his own company of horse, he was made the 1st Earl of Littlehampton of the second creation.

The new Earl's first action was to embark on the rebuilding of Drayneflete in a style more suited to his rank. For the house itself he called in Mr. Hawksmoor, who made short work of the old Elizabethan mansion, from which he retained only the Long Gallery. For the gardens he solicited the advice of the great Le Nôtre himself in Paris and for the decoration of the Great Saloon he relied on the talents of Sir James Thornhill. In the year that this great enterprise was finally completed he married Vanessa, only child and heiress of Sir Solomon Bunbury, Bt., a former Lord Mayor of London, possessed of vast estates in the West Indies.

'Il Magnifico', as he was commonly called by his contemporaries, in reference to his lavish personal expenditure coupled with a certain haughtiness of manner, while playing no very public part on the political stage, exercised a powerful influence behind the scenes. In the last years of Queen Anne's reign no man did more to counter the intrigues of Harley and Bolingbroke and to secure the Hanoverian succession. The importance of the role he played was fully realized by the new sovereign's advisers and in the Coronation Honours List he received, at long last, the Garter. In 1742 at the age of seventy-three he suffered a choleric seizure in his coach, provoked, so it is said, by the insolence of a toll-keeper to whom he was forced to take a horse-whip, and died before reaching home. He was survived by his wife and four children.

THE 1ST EARL OF LITTLEHAMPTON, K.G.
Sir James Thornhill

THE 1st Earl's marriage to the only daughter of the immensely wealthy Sir Solomon Bunbury, Bt., a Lord Mayor of London who, it was said, owned half the plantations in the West Indies, might well be described as 'à la mode', but thanks to the strength of character displayed by both parties the outcome was far removed from the dismal débâcle in which Hogarth's characters were involved. The bride, whose mother had been a Miss ffossil of Norfolk, inherited not only the beauty which had made that lady the Queen of the Swaffham Assembly Rooms but much of the energy which her grandfather had so successfully displayed in the management of his estates. Of the grandeur of her husband's position she was, from the first, fully appreciative and by her wit and by her social talents did much to enhance it. In Laroon's delightful canvas she is shown in mourning for her husband, who had died the previous year, and accompanied by her two daughters, Letitia and Euphemia with, in the background, her devoted page Hasdrubal, who had been born on her father's estate in Jamaica. This engaging blackamoor was held in the highest esteem by the whole family and his mistress took a particular pleasure in his company and insisted on his being always about her person. The Lady Letitia never married but, on the tragic death of her elder brother, devoted herself to the upbringing of her little nephew the 3rd Earl. The Lady Euphemia, on the other hand, whose irrepressible gaiety and strangely exotic beauty attracted innumerable suitors, survived three husbands: the 3rd Marquess of Tumbledown, who died in his seventy-eighth year, shortly after their marriage; Prince Ludwig of Kilmansegg-Lauterbach who fell at the Battle of Minden; and lastly Lord Jonathan Firturse who was killed in the hunting-field. The Countess herself lived on to welcome her grandson's first bride to Drayneflete and passed peacefully away at the faro table in 1772.

VANESSA, COUNTESS OF LITTLEHAMPTON
AND HER DAUGHTERS
Marcellus Laroon

WILLIAM, the 'Magnifico's' only son, cuts, perhaps inevitably, a rather dim figure alongside his illustrious parent. Not naturally gifted, what talents he possessed were not furthered by his education which, apart from a year or two at Winchester, took place largely in the stables and the servants' hall. However, it would be unwise unreservedly to accept the assertion made by Lord Hervey in his memoirs, that he was totally illiterate; abundant evidence exists in the Drayneflete muniment-room showing that he could write his own name very neatly. He remained a bachelor until after his succession to the title on his father's death, when he married a Miss Grosgrain who came, so it was claimed, from a very old Huguenot family. According to Hervey, who is clearly in this case a prejudiced source, he had first 'known' his bride when she was a fourteen-year-old still-room maid.

Although never commanding the immense respect in which his father had universally been held, the 2nd Earl was generally admitted to have been a superb horseman, a very capable Master of Hounds, and was very highly thought of in local cock-fighting circles. Not politically active, his only speech in the House of Lords, which has not alas survived, was described by a fellow peer as being 'incoherent but forthright'; he was a staunch upholder of the Hanoverian Succession and the Established Church, and his numerous pocket boroughs were always at the disposal of the Whigs. Happy in the place, if not the manner, of his death he was killed, at a comparatively early age, in a duel on Newmarket Heath by a certain Colonel Clapstock whose casual remarks on the parentage of his sister, the Lady Euphemia, he had much resented and whom he had, rather unwisely, challenged.

In Seymour's splendid canvas he is shown astride his celebrated stallion 'Hudibras' accompanied by his favourite bitch 'Clytie' from whom the whole of the existing Drayneflete pack directly descend.

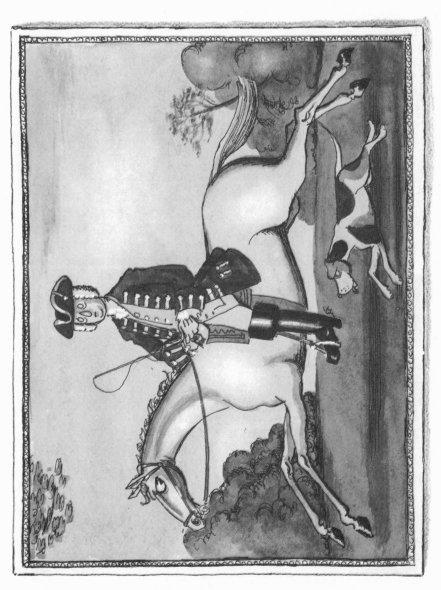

THE 2ND EARL OF LITTLEHAMPTON
James Seymour

THE YOUNGER of the two sons of the 1st Earl, who was born but a year before his father's death, was intended for a military career, but two events combined to change his vocation after he had served for only eighteen months in H.M. Foot Guards. First there seemed every likelihood that his regiment would be sent overseas, second, the incumbent of Coltsfoot Canonicorum, one of the best-endowed livings in his brother's gift, died unexpectedly. Accordingly he resigned his commission, went up to Pembroke College, Oxford, and took Holy Orders.

It might well be thought that a youth passed in the carefree atmosphere of St. James's would have proved an unpromising preparation for a clerical career, but such, it seems, was far from being the case. Joined to his brother's passion for rural sports was a fine literary taste and an enquiring mind and the young vicar was very soon contentedly settled in his remote parsonage. Within a year of his arrival he had excavated a Druidic dolmen in his kitchen garden of which in due course he published an illustrated account. This was followed first by *A Description of the Antiquities in the Hundred of Ballsoken* and some years later by *Hengist and Horsa*, a two thousand line poem in heroic couplets which achieved considerable contemporary success although little read today. Of the author Dr. Johnson is recorded as saying 'Sir, a man who can make so prodigious a brick with such a scant quantity of straw has a just claim to the amazed consideration of his fellows'.

In addition to his published works he kept a careful diary in which, under the date 4/IX/'78, occurs the following passage: 'Today my likeness by Mr. Stubbs came from the framemaker. I am well satisfied altho' methinks the cheeks are a little too full. Hannah, with the perversity of her sex, was enraptured by the painting of the house to the exclusion of all else. This evening had Squire Coltsfoot and a few friends to supper. All loud in their praise of Mr. Stubbs' genius. A good turbot, a dish of sweetbreads, a side of veal, two ducks, a saddle of lamb, sidedishes, and syllabubs.'

This estimable gentleman died in 1792 sincerely mourned by all his humble flock and by his many friends in the world of letters. He was survived by his widow – he had married his housekeeper in middle age – and an only son, Hengist, whose twin brother, Horsa, had died in infancy.

THE REVEREND THE HON. DR. LANCELOT DE COURANTSDAIR
George Stubbs

FROM his earliest youth – much to the distress of his parents – Hengist Courantsdair had been tainted with Enthusiasm. He frequented the company of Methodists and hedge-preachers and even in his schooldays was much given to Pentecostal outbursts. Some attributed this strange flaw in his character to his mother's side – it was rumoured that her grandfather had been, when young, a Fifth Monarchy man – others to the Huguenot influence of his aunt. Unfortunately this intemperate zeal was not confined to matters of religion, and he was soon notorious in the district for the loud expression of social and political views which could only be described as Jacobinical.

It was, therefore, not regarded as entirely a matter for regret when at the age of seventeen he ran away to America, the cause of whose newly liberated citizens he had always enthusiastically promoted. For many years nothing was heard, but by the end of the first decade of the new century, he was recorded as being established, having Anglicised his name, in Ipswich, Massachusetts, as a timber merchant. That his business was modestly successful is proved both by the existence of the old Coriander House on Argyla Road (now carefully preserved by the Ipswich Historical Society) and his marriage to a Hackenshaw of Newburyport.

With increasing prosperity his religious enthusiasm would seem to have taken second place to his commercial interests, although he was still regularly Moved by the Spirit to denounce the iniquities he saw flourishing around him. It is not recorded that he ever revisited the old country, but that all family ties were not completely broken is suggested by the presence in the Bequest of this charming example of the Primitive Art of the post-Colonial period.

His union was blessed by seventeen children of whom the most remarkable was Jethro, the third son. Obeying the contemporary injunction to 'go West' this young man founded the town of Littlehampton, Ohio, where he established a foundry, which supplied large quantities of cannon to the North during the war between the States (and if rumour is correct, quite a few to the South). From him the present head of the American branch of the family, Senator Jethro P. Coriander III, First President of The No Guaranty Trust of Philadelphia, of Consolidated Deterrents, of Napalm Products Inc., etc., etc., is directly descended.

HENGIST AND ABIGAIL CORIANDER
Artist unknown

BORN in 1749, the 3rd Earl succeeded his father at the age of twelve. His mother being rather slow-witted and a foreigner to boot, his early upbringing was largely entrusted to his aunt, Letitia, his father's unmarried sister. A bright and promising lad, he went to Merton College, Oxford, and thence on the Grand Tour, accompanied by one of the younger Fellows, the Reverend Doctor Fontwater. This proved to be the great formative experience of his life, and the enthusiasm for antiquity and the arts he then acquired was never abated. During his absence, and for months after his return, a constant stream of packing-cases was delivered at Drayne-flete containing Roman marbles and Greek vases, canvases by Salvator Rosa and Raphael Mengs, medieval manuscripts and Renaissance bronzes. As soon as these were installed he at once set about improving his surroundings, and called in Capability Brown to remodel the Park on the most approved modern principles. The lines of Le Nôtre's great avenues were ruthlessly twisted and broken; the formal canals were transformed into a chain of picturesque lakes; on every hillock well-sited elm clumps were planted, concealing grottoes and temples, and no vista lacked an eye-catching Folly. Immediately after his first marriage he decided the time had come to bring the house itself into conformity with its new setting. He therefore called in Mr. Wyatt, who made short work of Hawksmoor's pilasters and rustications and, by the introduction of pointed windows, crockets and castellations, restored to the ancient Abbey that ecclesiastical air which His Lordship's ancestors had been at such pains to banish. The changes were, however, largely external; inside, the Long Gallery, the only part of Sir Nicholas's original house to have survived, was carefully preserved and Thornhill's Great Saloon and the rest of the State Apartments were fortunately left untouched. However, a Gothic chapel was added to the south of the West Wing on what were thought to be the remains of the original abbey church but which recent research has shown to have been the site of the Abbot's wash-house.

In Reynolds's noble portrait the Earl is shown holding the plan of the excavations at Pozzuoli, carried out by the Dilettanti Society, of which he was a prominent member, and indicating the exact spot on which he himself found the celebrated bust of Scipio Africanus now in the British Museum.

THE 3RD EARL OF LITTLEHAMPTON
Sir Joshua Reynolds, P.R.A.

IN 1775 the 3rd Earl married Louisa, fourth daughter of the 2nd and last Duke of Buxton, a prominent member of the Whig Establishment. Her childhood had been sadly clouded by her father's disappointment at the Duchess's failure to produce an heir, which he did little to conceal from his wife or his offspring. This, acting on a nature prone to melancholy, had induced in her a permanent lowness of spirits which might well, given a husband less ebullient than the Earl, have rendered her marriage disastrous. But although they could never have been described as kindred spirits, she did her best to take an interest in her husband's artistic pursuits while he, concealing his irritation at her lifelong inability to distinguish between Correggio and Caravaggio, encouraged her efforts, never, alas, wholly successful, to master the harpsichord.

Her death, a year or two after the birth of their only child, Agatha, in 1782 filled him with genuine distress only partially assuaged by the erection of a magnificent mausoleum in the Saracenic style to his own designs.

It is said that on certain nights of the full moon a gentle rustle of silks is still heard passing down the Long Gallery, the door to the Green Drawing-Room opens and shuts of its own accord, and a moment or two later the midnight silence is softly broken by the strains of a particularly lugubrious aria from Handel's *Semele* rather tentatively played on one finger.

THE COUNTESS OF LITTLEHAMPTON
Thomas Gainsborough, R.A.

THE YOUNGER BROTHER of the 3rd Earl did not share, in any marked degree, the intellectual and cultural tastes for which his senior was justly renowned. Although he accompanied his brother on the Grand Tour, Venus rather than Minerva was always for him the favoured goddess, provoking his tutor to remark that 'if this devotion should continue unabated it is greatly to be feared 'twill only lead to a lifelong dependence on *MERCURY*'. A commission was therefore procured for him in one of His Majesty's ships of the line.

In the course of a long and distinguished career in the Senior Service his most notable exploit was undoubtedly the capture of Fort Shittipore, a strongly defended island in the Bay of Bengal, an achievement which was splendidly recorded in an enormous painting by John Singleton Copley, of which, alas, it has been possible to illustrate only a detail. Although the artist was not himself present at the battle, he spared no pains, as was his custom, to inform himself of every relevant detail before setting brush to canvas. Unfortunately, the long account of the action written by Major Flintlock, commanding the Marines (which is confirmed, incidentally, by the private diaries of the Reverend Doctor Fontwater who was serving as Chaplain to the expedition) was not at that time readily available. According to this, the attack was launched at dawn, the fort finally falling at 11 in the forenoon, and the Admiral did not himself come ashore until shortly before sundown.

Having, as a result of this victory, acquired a very considerable sum in prize-money and the ribbon of the Bath (which by a curious oversight on the part of the artist he is here shown wearing some eighteen months before the award was in fact made) he retired from the Service, married the Hon. Lavinia Ballcock, the eldest daughter of Admiral the Viscount Bulwark, and purchased a fine estate in the neighbourhood of Sidmouth, rebuilding the house, which he renamed Shittipore, in the Hindu style to the designs of Sir William Chambers. He died at a very advanced age leaving seventeen children, none born in wedlock.

THE CAPTURE OF FORT SHITTIPORE [*a detail*]
John Singleton Copley

JOSEPH GRUMBLE came of what is euphemistically described as good yeoman stock. As a lad his appearance was engaging and his intelligence well above the average and he soon attracted the attention of the local parson who not only saw to it that he received a rather better education than other boys of his rank in life but, when adolescence was past, obtained for him a clerkship in the East India Company. The good old man's generosity was abundantly rewarded, for Joseph was never a man to neglect his opportunities and within a very short time he was well established as an Assistant Inspector of Taxes in the State of Buggeribad. Fulfilling his official duties with competence and regularity he nevertheless had sufficient time on his hands to go into jute and, to a lesser extent, teak and spices, and had by the age of thirty-five amassed a very considerable fortune which increased annually. By the time that William Hickey came to Madras he was installed in one of the finest houses of the town and maintained a state second only to that of the Governor himself.

He was married three times, but the rigours of the climate, by which he himself appeared to be quite unaffected, proved too great and all his wives predeceased him, as indeed did all his children save Louisa, his youngest daughter by his third wife. In Zoffany's fine canvas, painted in 1786, shortly before the old man's final retirement, he is shown on the veranda of his great house surrounded by his servants and accompanied by his little daughter. In little more than a year after the picture was completed both were back in England comfortably installed in the splendid estate of Drayneflete Magna, only a stone's throw from the Abbey, which he had at once acquired.

It is interesting to record that the little girl's faithful *ayah*, shown on the extreme right in the picture, accompanied her young mistress back to England where she was soon converted to the true faith, became a prominent member of the Countess of Huntingdon's Connection, and married an eminent shipschandler in Bristol.

JOSEPH GRUMBLE ESQ.

J. Zoffany, R.A.

WHEN Joseph Grumble on retirement established himself as a country gentleman it seems likely that his choice of residence was guided by the 3rd Earl of Littlehampton's younger brother, with whom he had established a firm friendship when the Admiral was on the East India station. It is beyond doubt that this old association was responsible for the friendly relationship which rapidly developed between the neighbouring landowners. At this time the 3rd Earl was beginning to find widowerhood irksome and it is hardly surprising that the Nabob's little daughter, a remarkably early developer, should have attracted his friendly notice. Moreover he could hardly have been unaware, as the bills for all his architectural improvements steadily mounted, of the immense fortune she was likely to inherit. It was, therefore, no surprise to their intimates when, on her fifteenth birthday, Miss Grumble, with her father's blessing, and a large settlement, became Countess of Littlehampton. To the world at large, however, this love-match quickly became a topic for eager, and not invariably kindly, speculation. 'Has His Lordship told you, madam', writes Horace Walpole to the Countess Ossory, 'of Lord Littlehampton's affecting romance. . . ? Juliet it appears is not much more than five-and-thirty years junior to Romeo but I suppose the latter judged the young lady's jointure far outweighed the exertion of scaling a balcony. The thought of what he will do with all those lakhs of rupees is beyond my conjuring. The last time I was in that part of the country his park was so full of whimsical additions that you could not see the wood for the pagodas. The Nabob is said to be mightily pleased. Whether Iphigenia considers a coronet sufficient recompense for her sacrifice is only to be guessed at.'

Horace Walpole need not have worried; the young bride is reported to have manifested the greatest enthusiasm for her new role, and it was not long before her wit, beauty and vivacity became the talk of the town. Within two years the happiness of her indulgent spouse was crowned by the birth of two boys. As soon as she had fully recovered the Earl, taking advantage of a temporary lull in European hostilities, set off with a numerous train to familiarize the young Countess with the wonders of his beloved Rome. It was on this occasion that he commissioned the celebrated Canova to immortalize her beauty in marble.

THE COUNTESS OF LITTLEHAMPTON
Canova

WITHIN less than a year of the death of the Earl, his Countess, who was still a young woman, married the Hon. Sysonby Flannel, the second son of the 3rd Viscount Cheddar, an Ensign in H.M. Foot Guards. Their union was idyllic but brief, the gallant bridegroom falling at Corunna, whereupon, after a due period of mourning, his widow was joined in wedlock to Sir Tresham Manifest, Bt., H.M. Minister Plenipotentiary in Stockholm, whom she duly accompanied to the Congress of Vienna where he was number two in the British delegation. In 1815, on the very eve of the final session, the world learnt with astonishment that Her Ladyship had bolted with General Prince Goloshkin, an A.D.C. to the Tsar, leaving her husband with their eighteen-month-old son. The scandal was immense and the guilty pair went into exile in the Ottoman Empire. After a time, however, the Tsar's wrath abated and the Prince, now legally married, was permitted to take up an attachment at the Russian Mission to the Sublime Porte.

It was in the course of an official visit to the Holy Land that the Prince's party were overwhelmed by a band of marauding Arabs in the neighbourhood of Damascus. The Prince barely escaped with his life and his wife was carried off to adorn the harem of the leader. For some years nothing more was heard of the Princess, and then travellers' tales of a beautiful European lady, the principal wife of an immensely rich Alawit Sheikh, who was presiding over a miniature court in a handsome castle in the mountains behind Latakia, began to filter back. Soon a regular flow of European pilgrims to the Holy Land turned up at her residence; all reported that, although no longer young, the former Countess had retained all her remembered beauty and fascination. She soon became known as the 'Ninon de l'Enclos du Levant' and so powerless was age to wither her charms that it is reported that, when in her seventies, she successfully seduced Mr. Holman Hunt on the shores of the Dead Sea, thus delaying the completion of *The Scapegoat* by several weeks. The exact date of her death is unrecorded but she was buried beneath an elegant *turbeh* on the heights overlooking the B'qaa which remains to this day a popular place of pilgrimage for devout Alawits.

THE HON.
SYSONBY
FLANNEL
Artist
unknown

PRINCE GOLOSHKIN
Daffinger

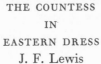

THE COUNTESS
IN
EASTERN DRESS
J. F. Lewis

SIR TRESHAM MANIFEST, BT.
After Lawrence

SHEIKH ABD'L BOUBA
Qajar School

THE ELDER SON of the 3rd Earl was, from all accounts, cursed with a strangely unsettled character; inheriting his mother's passionate nature (although, not, alas, her looks) without her shrewdness, his father's extravagant bent was not, in him, redeemed by those artistic tastes which had earned the 3rd Earl the soubriquet of 'Sensibility'. He was renowned for his wit, of which Captain Gronow has in his memoirs recorded a characteristic example. At a party at Carlton House, meeting with a Duchess celebrated for her massive charms, he seized an arum lily from a near-by vase and plunging it into her corsage remarked, 'Allow me, madam. A lily for your valley!' – a pleasantry which earned him exclusion from Almack's for a whole year.

Even in the Regent's circle his capacity for hard liquors was conspicuous and the same diarist informs us that he was accustomed to consume brandy and orange curaçao 'in quantities fearful to behold'. His successes with the fair sex were legendary, of which that which excited the greatest envy among his contemporaries was his seduction of the fifteen-year-old Carlotta Cannelloni, whose affections he retained for a number of years. This remarkable girl, in whose company he is shown in the accompanying plate, early in life displayed a soprano voice of quite extraordinary power and range which her protector arranged to be trained by the most admired masters of the day, with such success that a few years after this likeness was taken she enjoyed a memorable success at Drury Lane creating the role of Elfrida in *La Muette de Portici*, and continued to enrapture vast audiences in all the opera-houses of Europe for more than thirty years.

His end was tragic; on leaving a splendid banquet in the Pavilion celebrating the Regent's birthday he insisted, against all advice, on driving himself back to his lodgings. The night was foggy and he had the misfortune to drive himself and his curricle off the end of the chain pier. His horse had the good luck – or the sagacity – to swim ashore, but the 4th Earl made his last public appearance a few days later in a fisherman's net off Bexhill.

Note. The accompanying hand-coloured engraving is attributed in the Littlehampton Catalogue to Gillray, but I can find no reference to it in the authoritative and exhaustive volumes which Mr. Draper Hill of Boston has devoted to the master. Moreover, the Brighton Pavilion was only completed in its present form in 1811, a date by which Gillray, who died in 1815, had almost ceased to practise his art.

'BEAU LITTLEHAMPTON'

From a contemporary engraving by Gillray [?]

JOSEPH, who succeeded to the Earldom on the tragic death of his elder brother, was a man of very different stamp. Serious-minded and public-spirited, he spoke frequently, and at length, in the Upper House. However, despite his loyalty to the Whigs and his support for the Reform Bill, which involved the disappearance of the two-member constituency of Coltsfoot, the most profitable of his pocket boroughs, public office always eluded him; by how narrow a margin is revealed in the following letter from Creevey: 'Dined with the Seftons, also there Wickedshifts, Sydney Smith, Lambton and "Pomposo" Littlehampton. The last refused to speak to Wickedshifts whom he regards as being responsible for his being out of office. Apparently he was confidently expecting the Admiralty and was furious at being offered Woods and Forests, without a seat in the Cabinet. After Wickedshifts had left he explained to me and Sefton how well suited he was to the former post as his uncle had been an admiral! Was there ever?!'

After this setback the Earl devoted himself largely to his arboretum and local affairs and as a J.P. and later Lord-Lieutenant (in the uniform of which high office he was painted by Winterhalter) earned for himself the unstinted admiration of all his neighbours. He still appeared in the Upper House from time to time, when the Whigs could always rely on his vote, and usually a long and cogently argued speech justifying his support for whatever government measure was under discussion. This unswerving devotion to Whig principles did not pass unnoticed and Lord Melbourne, during his second administration, made him a Privy Councillor, in which capacity he attended the historic meeting on the accession of Queen Victoria. He died of an apoplectic fit while reviewing the Volunteers on Drayneflete Common in 1865 and was succeeded by his only son who at once inherited the Earldom, but had to wait for some years yet for his mother's Barony.

Today the 5th Earl is chiefly remembered for the *Cupressus putrescens*, or Littlehamptonia, as it is popularly called, which was first raised in Drayneflete Park.

THE 5TH EARL OF LITTLEHAMPTON
F. X. Winterhalter

THE 5TH COUNTESS was born Dorothea MacStruth, the only child of Sir Alistair MacStruth, Bt., and Lady Lochwhistle of Lochwhistle, a Baroness in her own right. From both parents she inherited large estates in Scotland and from her mother the Barony.

Brought up as a strict Presbyterian, she displayed, even as a young woman, a remarkable firmness of character which did not escape the notice of Mr. Creevey: 'Went to Holland House where I found a large party including "Pomposo" and his bride. The latter a formidable, fine-looking young person – another Lieven – if you can imagine *that* lady with a Scots accent and a Presbyterian conscience! Old Madagascar in one of her worst moods, but the Hieland Lassie gave as good as she got. "Pomposo" his usual self. When I said in my last letter that Lord Tullamore was the greatest bore in London I was wrong!'

The Countess's character did not soften with the years. While remaining a staunch Presbyterian north of the Border, in London she gave her full support to the Evangelical wing of the Established Church, was a regular patroness of revivalist meetings in Exeter Hall and a leading figure in the Temperance Movement. Her dominance of her husband was, in later life, absolute. As previously recorded she clothed and removed to the servants' hall Cranach's splendid *Cleopatra* and she it was who banished into outer darkness Canova's superb statue of her mother-in-law, whose very name could not be mentioned in her hearing. Only when she ordered all his French brandy to be poured down the sink is it recorded that the Earl made his single, but ineffectual, protest. With her daughter-in-law, whose marriage she had done so much to promote, her relations were never easy; mistrustful of her artistic activities she was scandalized by her Tractarian leanings, and after a monumental row on the vexed subject of the Eastward Position the two ladies never again exchanged a word.

THE COUNTESS OF LITTLEHAMPTON
F. X. Winterhalter

AS THE YEARS went on the 5th Earl became increasingly worried by the predicament of his half-sister, his father's child by his first wife. This lady lacked not only those superficial charms likely to attract suitors of her own rank but was wholly dependent on the generosity of her half-brother. It was, therefore, with a cheerful and uncharacteristic disregard for social distinctions that he gave his consent to her marriage to the Reverend Aloysius Fontwater, a penniless curate and youngest of the eleven children of old Dr. Fontwater, the 3rd Earl's tutor. By great good fortune the living of Coltsfoot Canonicorum had been left, ever since the death of the Reverend the Hon. Lancelot, in charge of a curate who was now replaced by the Reverend Fontwater. A year or two later, through the influence of an uncle on his mother's side, who was the Senior Warden of the Worshipful Company of Drumstretchers, he was presented with the important and well-endowed living of St. Ursula-inside-the-Wardrobe. Very shortly afterwards he became a Prebendary of St. Pauls.

A staunch middle-of-the-road man, his contempt for the Evangelicals was only exceeded by his detestation of the Puseyites; an eloquent preacher with powerful Whig connections, it was clear that the Reverend Aloysius had a great future ahead of him, and his appointment to the See of Barnstaple, caused no surprise. Soon after his induction, however, the new Bishop became involved in one of the great ecclesiological controversies of the period. His cathedral, in a poor state of repair, was due to be rebuilt and the work had been entrusted to Mr. Butterfield, a notorious Tractarian. The Bishop immediately cancelled the contract only to discover that he had acted *ultra vires* as the decision rested with the Dean and Chapter who insisted firmly on their rights. However, they had sadly underestimated their man. Before he knew where he was the unfortunate Dean found himself up before the Consistory Court to answer charges of simony, rejection of the doctrine of Baptismal Regeneration and misappropriation of the Easter Offering. The Archbishop was forced to intervene and finally the Bishop withdrew the charges and the Chapter agreed to replace Mr. Butterfield by Sir Gilbert Scott. Dr. Fontwater was the last bishop regularly to wear a wig in the House of Lords.

THE RIGHT REVEREND BISHOP FONTWATER
From an engraving by J. Phillips

THE LADY AGATHA FONTWATER
Artist unknown

ALISTAIR, the son and heir of 'Pomposo', was described by the more indulgent of his relatives as a 'child of nature'. Never happier then when in the company of dumb animals, as a lad he spent far more hours in the kennels than in the schoolroom. Born into a humbler rank of society he would have made an admirable vet and, indeed, among his Highland neighbours he was regarded as the leading authority on softpad.

His parents, however, felt that this specialized talent would not of itself equip him to manage his estates, and had soon regretfully to recognize that he possessed no other. This was the more serious as the 5th Earl was himself financially embarrassed. His father's building activities had made serious inroads on the Littlehampton fortune, his mother's vast Grumble inheritance she had taken with her on re-marriage, and he was for long burdened by the necessity of discharging his late brother's enormous debts.

It was not surprising, therefore, that when Sir Ebenezer Horseferry acquired the estate adjoining Lochwhistle the Countess should have cast a speculative eye on her neighbour's daughters. Great was her joy when it became apparent that Alistair regarded the fair Louisa with an affectionate interest almost as great as that aroused by his Labrador bitch.

The resultant marriage was not unhappy. True the husband spent most of the year on his Scottish estates while the wife always passed the whole season in London; nevertheless they enjoyed sufficient time in each other's company to produce eight children. In his wife's artistic activities the Earl took no interest, although he did consent to sit to Sir Edwin Landseer, the only artist for whom he ever expressed any admiration, for his portrait, while the Countess who had inherited her father's taste along with his collection, as well as her mother's musical talents, shunned the moors and devoted herself to stalking Pre-Raphaelites in Cheyne Walk.

In 1889 the Earl was so unfortunate as to be knocked out by a falling ptarmigan of exceptional size, an accident from which he never fully recovered, dying the following year. He was survived by his widow who passed peacefully away, while reading Dante on the terrace of her lovely villa above Fiesole, some few years later.

THE 6TH EARL OF LITTLEHAMPTON
Sir Edwin Landseer, R.A.

IN THE LATTER HALF of the 18th century there flourished, in the little town of Muddlesborough in the North Riding, a young blacksmith named Jonas Horseferry. Largely self-taught, but exceptionally shrewd, he recognized sooner than most the nature of the great change that was then taking place in rural industry, enlarged his forge, set up a smelting-yard and by the turn of the century had become one of the most successful ironmasters in the county. He married, in the year of Trafalgar, the daughter of a local Methodist minister who duly presented him with a son and heir, Ebenezer.

Thanks to his mother Ebenezer received a rather better education than his father whose partner he soon became. Under his direction the family business expanded fourfold and when in 1837 he married a daughter of the manse, he brought his bride home not to the modest farmhouse on the hills above the town, where his father had recently died, but to a splendid mansion in the Jacobethan style which the genius of Mr. Salvin had caused to arise on the site. With the coming of the railways his already large fortune vastly increased and encouraged by his wife, a woman of wide culture, he was in a position to indulge his enthusiasm for the arts to the full. At the same time he acquired a fine town mansion in the newly developed Kensington Palace Gardens and an estate in Scotland.

It was not, therefore, surprising that in 1851 he should have been nominated one of the Commissioners for the Great Exhibition. So enthusiastically did he address himself to his task that he was rewarded not only with a baronetcy but also with the close friendship of the Prince Consort.

In this charming watercolour by Mulready he is shown in the company of his wife, a most talented pianist who later became a close friend of Liszt, his elder daughter, Laura, who never married but who, under the name of Roderick Gunwale, was to achieve such fame as the author of a series of three-volume novels of naval life as to earn for herself the title of the 'Queen of Mudie's', and, on his knee, his younger daughter, the future Countess of Littlehampton.

SIR EBENEZER HORSEFERRY, BT. AND FAMILY
William Mulready, R.A.

THE ELDEST DAUGHTER of the 6th Earl was very much her mother's child; of her father's enthusiasm for the outdoor life and the animal creation she showed no trace, but the artistic tastes, so long cultivated in the maternal line, she inherited to the full. The 6th Countess was on terms of delighted intimacy with many members of the Pre-Raphaelite circle and her beloved child was painted not only by Rossetti, who described her as 'a regular stunner', but also by Burne-Jones, Walter Crane, G. F. Watts (twice) and Sir Frank Dicksee. It was, however, a passion for music which dominated her early years; at that time the work of the Elizabethan composers was little known and it was to her researches that much of its later popularity was largely due. A founder-member of the Madrigal Society, her collection of sackbuts (now in the Metropolitan Museum in New York) was unique.

Curiously enough it was indirectly due to her musical interests that, in middle life, she played that prominent role in public affairs for which she is chiefly remembered. Thanks to her close friendship with Dame Ethel Smythe she embraced, shortly after the turn of the century, the cause of Women's Suffrage with all the passionate enthusiasm of her nature. Of her many well-publicized efforts in support of the cause, the most noteworthy was her gallant action in chaining herself to the railings of White's Club, albeit there were those who said that the avowed motive of the demonstration – to secure the release from Wormwood Scrubs of Mrs. Pankhurst – perhaps took second place to a keen desire to embarrass her brother, a prominent member of the Committee. At the same time the deeply mystical strain in her character was satisfied by her friendship with Mrs. Besant and membership of the Theosophical Society.

On the outbreak of the First World War her support for the Allied cause was whole-hearted, in marked contrast to her attitude in the previous conflict when she had been vociferously pro-Boer, and she was tireless in organizing concerts of 17th-century music for the troops. After the war she paid a long visit to India and came back a practising Buddhist and a skilled performer on the sitar. She never married and died very suddenly in 1924, overwhelmed by emotion, in the front row of the stalls at a matineé performance of *The Immortal Hour*.

66

'FLORA'

D. G. Rossetti

COSMO, the second child and eldest son of the 6th Earl, was educated at Eton and Christ Church, Oxford. As a young man he sat for several years as Liberal Member for Drayneflete, but he always had reservations about his leader and was unalterably opposed to Home Rule so that his translation to the Lords on the death of his father was for him a welcome release. Thereafter, when in London, he passed rather more time at Marlborough House than at Westminster. While inheriting his father's sporting tastes to the full, Newmarket rather than Lochwhistle was always his Mecca, but unfortunately despite the large number of horses he had in training, the more glittering prizes of the Turf invariably escaped him. Of his mother's artistic tastes he showed few signs, although he is known to have had a fondness for the music of Meyerbeer and was reported once to have expressed an admiration for the paintings of Rosa Bonheur. He had, while at Oxford, gained the reputation of being one of the best whist-players in the University but unfortunately he was never able in later life fully to master the intricacies of baccarat. This strange disability, combined with his persistent ill-luck on the race-course, so seriously embarrassed his finances that by the early 1890s matrimony seemed likely to provide the only solution. Normally irresolute, in a crisis the Earl always reacted swiftly and without hesitation and on the 1st of June 1892 he was joined in holy wedlock, in the sight of the most fashionable congregation which even St. George's, Hanover Square, had ever known, to Miss Miriam Truffelheim of Frankfurt, only child of that well-known financier and international sportsman, Baron Truffelheim (later Sir Sigismund Truffelheim, K.C.V.O.). The Prince of Wales was best man and the honeymoon was spent at Biarritz.

'A SEASIDE SWELL'
Carlo Pellegrini

FEW EPISODES in the Second Matabele Campaign excited such popular enthusiasm as the charge of the 27th Light Dragoons at Bhanwhana, led by Captain (as he then was) Frederick Courantsdair, second son of the 6th Earl of Littlehampton. This historic engagement, from which the Captain, thanks largely to his splendid mount, alone escaped unscathed, was duly immortalized in a noble canvas by Lady Butler (12 ft. by $7\frac{1}{2}$ ft.), that once hung in the billiard-room at Drayneflete but which has for some years been on loan to the Cavalry Club.* The Captain's subsequent career proved fully worthy of its auspicious opening. In the Boer War he served with distinction on the staff of General Buller, was Second-in-Command of the rear column at the Relief of Mafeking and ended the campaign as a full Colonel. In August 1914, on learning of the German ultimatum, he immediately abandoned the mutiny he was helping to organize at the Curragh and reported at once to his old friend Sir Henry Wilson and was duly appointed Second-in-Command of the 3rd Cavalry Division, taking over the command early in 1915. Throughout the following terrible years he never once lost his faith in ultimate victory and always managed in the face of appalling difficulties to keep his beloved cavalry in tip-top shape waiting for the final breakthrough. When at last this came, so impetuous was his advance through the enemy lines that, as one of his close companions-in-arms remarked at the time, 'it was dam' lucky for Freddy that the referee blew his whistle when he did'.

After the war he served in India, Egypt and as G.O.C. Northern Command, retiring with rank of full General in 1933.

On the outbreak of the last war, he at once offered his services to the War Office, but after a short spell in the military censorship retired to devote himself full time to the organization and command of the Drayneflete Home Guard. In this role his most notable exploit was the disposal of a large unexploded bomb which fell in the middle of the Common which he insisted, brushing aside his Sergeant-Major's protests, in defusing himself. The enormous crater which resulted was subsequently laid out as a Memorial Bog Garden, at the expense of the present Earl who presented it to the town at a simple service of dedication, conducted by Canon Fontwater, on the fifth anniversary of his uncle's death.

*Where it is likely to remain. R.S.

'THE LAST CHARGE OF THE 27TH' [*a detail*]
Lady Butler

THE SECOND and favourite daughter of the 6th Earl shared all her male parent's tastes to the full. As soon as she was out of the nursery her days were spent either in the stables or the kennels. Although an accomplished and vigorous performer in eightsome reels, of her mother's deep love of music she showed no further sign, and her appreciation of the fine arts was strictly limited to the works of Sartorius and Sir Francis Grant. A superb horsewoman, her exploits, not only with the Drayneflete, but also with the Quorn, the Pytchley and the Galway Blazers, were legendary. In 1893 she married Colonel Sir Jasper Wickham-Stench, Bt., sometime joint Master of the Bicester. The marriage, although unblessed with offspring, was a complete success, but unfortunately the Colonel, who was some years her senior, and whose health had been weakened by prolonged service on the North-West Frontier, predeceased her by many years. 'I am rather afraid', she used frequently to remark, 'that poor dear Jasper was not quite up to my weight.'

The accompanying portrait was presented to her by followers of the Drayneflete at a moving ceremony at the New Year's Meet in 1935 when she celebrated the fiftieth anniversary of her first appearance with the pack and her twenty-fifth as Master. During the last war, when most of her own, and as much as she could lay hands on of her household's, rations went straight to the kennels, she not only managed to hunt twice a week but, with a view to saving petrol, also organized and commanded a mounted squadron of the W.V.S. which did sterling work, delivering 'meals on wheels' at a far greater speed and over a much larger area than would have been possible on foot. Her end was blissful; she died, if not in harness, at least in the harness-room, where she collapsed into the arms of the whipper-in after consuming a friendly glass of cherry brandy to celebrate the new litter to which her favourite bitch had just given birth. She was in her eighty-second year and her last words, very strongly spoken, were 'Gone away!'

THE LADY AGATHA WICKHAM-STENCH
Sir Alfred Munnings, P.R.A.

THE YOUNGEST of the three sons of the 6th Earl was, when young, handicapped by ill-health. After a very short period at Eton he had to be removed to warmer climes and was educated privately until he went up to Brasenose College, Oxford, where he came under the influence of Mr. Walter Pater. After two formative years he came down without taking a degree, and was thenceforth to be found at the centre of that artistic circle presided over by his mother, or at the Café Royal. An occasional contributor to *The Yellow Book*, he also published a beautifully produced volume of translations of Pierre Louÿs and a slim volume of poems, some of which were set to music by his friend Reynaldo Hahn.

In the spring of 1895 he left, rather suddenly, for abroad and from then on resided permanently at the charming villa inherited from his mother above Fiesole which his exquisite hospitality and informed taste rendered a place of pilgrimage for three generations of art-lovers. In the Florentine social life of the day he played a notable role, enjoying the friendship of Vernon Lee, Lucie Duff Gordon, Ouida, Bernard Berenson and Mrs. Keppel, although, curiously enough, never being on speaking terms with more than two of them at any one time.

On the outbreak of the last war he was forced to abandon his beloved Florence and take refuge with his niece-by-marriage, the present Countess, who kindly gave him shelter at Drayneflete. Here, despite the close proximity of his brother Frederick and a company of A.T.S. stationed in the Abbey, both of which he found uncongenial, he settled down quite happily, occupying his leisure with the production of an exquisite *petit-point* carpet (now in the Green Drawing-Room) which he laughingly referred to as 'my war-work'.

On the cessation of hostilities he returned at once to the Villa Dolce which he found neglected but mercifully undamaged, and where ten years later he died in his sleep. To his niece, for whom he had developed a warm affection, he left his portrait by Boldini and his celebrated collection of Fabergé Easter eggs. The remainder of his estate passed to his faithful valet Alfredo.

THE HON. ALGERNON COURANTSDAIR
Boldini

IN the Royal Academy Exhibition of 1881 the Picture of the Year was unquestionably *Pussy's Going Bye-Byes* by the President himself; universally acclaimed, even Mr. Ruskin could not withhold his admiration, which in the circumstances was magnanimous, declaring it to be the equal of the finest work of Kate Greenaway and Fra Angelico.

The original of this charming study of childhood was the Lady Ethel, youngest child of the 6th Earl of Littlehampton, who had inherited to the full her father's love of all forms of animal life. Generally acknowledged to be the most beautiful débutante of 1897 it was confidently expected that she would make a brillant match. Alas, it was not to be! A highly romantic nature and High Church leanings led her to reject all her numerous suitors and to fall hopelessly in love with a penniless curate at All Saints, Margaret Street. Her brother, a staunch Evangelical, was at first firmly opposed to any idea of marriage but even when, under his mother's influence, he had been induced to give his grudging consent, the course of true love did not run smooth. During a protracted engagement the bridegroom-to-be struggled manfully with his conscience and his vicar, who held strong views on clerical celibacy; but shortly before coming to a final decision, never robust and exhausted by this inner conflict, he succumbed to the influenza epidemic then raging.

For the Lady Ethel the blow was severe and for a time she contemplated entering an Anglican sisterhood. Finally dissuaded by her family from so drastic a step, she thenceforth devoted her life to good works. Naturally it was animal welfare which excited her keenest enthusiasm – lost dogs and stray cats never had so doughty a champion, and many a Littlehampton water-trough still testifies to her solicitude for cart-horses – but her compassion knew no limits and was freely extended to Distressed Gentlefolk, Sons of the Clergy and Fallen Women. No woman of her generation organized more tombolas or opened more bazaars, and in 1911 she was appointed Lady-in-Waiting to H.R.H. Princess Marie Louise.

Today, well on in her tenth decade, she still presides over innumerable committees in her house in Cadogan Square, which she refused to leave even during the height of the Blitz, surrounded by four Pekinese, six Siamese cats, a score of budgerigars and a parrot.

'PUSSY'S GOING BYE-BYES'
Sir John Everett Millais, Bt. P.R.A.

MISS MIRIAM TRUFFELHEIM was the only daughter of Baron Truffelheim, the financial genius who reorganized the K.u.K. Eisenbahn Gesellschaft, established the Bosnia-Herzegovina Handelsbank and was ennobled by the Emperor Franz Josef. An intimate friend of H.R.H. the Prince of Wales, as was his daughter, the Baron, having previously adopted British nationality, was created K.C.V.O. in the Coronation Honours List. At the same time he acquired substantial interests in Johannesburg. His daughter, whose wit and beauty had created something of a sensation when she was launched on London Society at a great ball in her father's residence in Park Lane, soon took her place alongside Daisy, Princess of Pless, Lady Warwick and Mrs. Cornwallis-West as one of the toasts of the town without whom no smart house-party could be considered a success.

Once established in the old Littlehampton House in St. James's Square, the new Countess promptly embarked on a social career of dazzling brilliance; balls, routs and supper-parties followed each other in quick succession and during the shooting season the Abbey was the scene of many a high-spirited gathering. Possessed of a robust sense of humour and a gift for mimicry, she was the organizer of innumerable practical jokes, of which, perhaps, the most celebrated was the occasion when she donned a false moustache and a monocle and won the egg-and-spoon race at the Vicarage Fête in the character of Monsieur de Soveral. Another time, disguised as an old gipsy-woman, she went round an Ascot house-party reading palms; unfortunately in reading Mrs. Keppel's she proved a little too accurate and for a time her relations with her sovereign were characterized by an unusual coolness.

When, after the birth of her only daughter, it became clear that all hope of an heir must be abandoned, the Earl and Countess gradually drifted apart and it was no surprise when in 1905 they separated by mutual agreement. Thenceforward the Countess spent much of her time in her beautiful villa on Cap Ferrat, marrying first, Prince Annibale Brutafigura (marriage dissolved 1921) and then Hiram van Stickleback III, the well-known international yachtsman, on whose Long Island estate she died in 1943.

MIRIAM, COUNTESS OF LITTLEHAMPTON

J. S. Sargent, R.A.

THE BREAK-UP of his first marriage in 1905 was a source of considerable distress to the 7th Earl and in the late summer of that year he went for a couple of weeks, before the grouse season opened, to take the restorative waters of Harrogate. While there he made the acquaintance of a Miss Lottie Dolores (*née* Bloggs) of Tulse Hill who was appearing in the No. 2 touring company of *San Toy*. Acquaintance ripened into friendship, friendship into love, and in the following spring they were joined in wedlock.

The bride was the daughter of one of the most respected publicans in South London and her mother had, in her youth, gained a modest but deserved fame by being shot from a cannon twice nightly at the Westminster Aquarium. Many of the Earl's acquaintances were sceptical about the future happiness of a pair with such widely differing backgrounds, but they were soon rebuked. The new Countess, who had inherited much of her father's business sense, at once set about bringing order into the 7th Earl's rather confused finances, and she handled his dependants and the domestic staff on his various estates with the same firmness that had gained her the ungrudging respect of the patrons of the Saloon Bar at the Plumbers' Arms where she had, from time to time, been accustomed to help out while 'resting'.

Early in 1906 she gave birth to a daughter and in the following year the longed-for heir. Outside her family her main interests were the Conservative Party and charity; the former made Littlehampton House, in St. James's Square, one of the principal rallying-points of the stern, unbending Tories during the constitutional crisis of 1911, the latter gained her the close friendship of her sister-in-law the Lady Ethel who, when it came to arranging charity matinées, found her experience invaluable. Only once, however, did she herself ever again perform in public, and then involuntarily; at a great Victory Bonds rally at the Albert Hall in 1916 she stepped into the gap left by Dame Clara Butt (who had had the misfortune to be knocked down by a Boy Scout on a bicycle during a Zeppelin raid the night before) and led a wildly enthusiastic audience in the singing of 'Keep the Home Fires Burning'.

She survived her husband by many years, dying early in 1952, universally mourned; at her memorial service at St. Paul's Knightsbridge it was standing room only.

'OURSELVES AND TUM-TUM' – DRAYNEFLETE, CHRISTMAS 1904

CHARLOTTE, COUNTESS OF LITTLEHAMPTON
ON HER MARRIAGE   AT THE CORONATION
                      OF H.M. KING GEORGE VI

THE 7th EARL'S only daughter by his first marriage was christened Mabel, a name which she intensely disliked and for which, when she came out shortly after the First World War, she substituted Amethyst. In the London of the roaring 'twenties few roared louder than she; a ring-leader of the Bright Young People, no party was complete without her and her own entertainments, often given, much to the annoyance of her stepmother, in Littlehampton House, invariably made the headlines. Of these the most celebrated, indeed notorious, was the Bible Ball where all the guests came as characters from Holy Writ with the hostess, predictably, as Salome. Unfortunately the evening ended disastrously when 'Togo' Staplehurst, who had come as St. Paul, fell out of the basket in which he was being lowered from a third-storey window and broke his neck. Shortly after this she abandoned London for a while, to the unconcealed delight of the Countess, for an apartment in the Rue du Bac, where she soon gathered round her a band of artistic and distinguished friends. She smoked opium with Cocteau, played duets with Poulenc and was dressed by Coco Chanel, gaining for herself the affectionate nickname of 'La Vache sur le Toit'.

However, despite her Parisian success, she did not neglect her old friends and commuted to London regularly during the Season, and it was there that she first encountered Evelyn Waugh who has left a vivid account of the meeting in his recently published diaries: 'After dinner went on to party of *****. Everyone beastly drunk. Bruno Hat and some filthy dago sodomizing on the sofa. Found myself next to a Lesbian friend of Hamish, whom I at once suspected of being a flagellant, who bored me to death talking about people in Paris I didn't know. However, when Hamish told me she was Willy Drayneflete's half-sister, decided to accept her offer of a lift home. Discovered in the cab that she was not a Lesbian but was a whipper. Woke up sore and exhausted and had to go straight round to White's for a couple of brandies-and-crême-de-menthes.'

The year following this entry, she was married in Paris to a well-known interior decorator, the Marquis de Pernod-Framboise.

The Marquise predeceased her husband by several years, dying in 1940 as a result of a rather mysterious car smash after a late-night party in Nairobi.

'LADY A á LONGCHAMPS'
Van Dongen

URSULA, the elder child of the 7th Earl's second marriage, inherited her paternal grandmother's artistic enthusiasm in full measure. This, together with the markedly unconventional streak which she displayed when still a child, while giving no satisfaction to her mother, at once endeared her to her Aunt Flora, who not only encouraged her artistic ambitions but paid for her to study at the Slade. Social life she scorned and only attended débutante dances under maternal pressure and the sole country-house she could be induced to visit was, occasionally, Garsington. All the Countess's efforts to encourage her daughter to conform to a way of life suitable to her rank were finally thwarted on the death of the Lady Flora who left her niece the whole of her fortune, thus enabling her to set herself up in a large studio in Fitzroy Square. Like her benefactress, she developed, as time went on, a keen interest in social questions and during the 1930s she marched in countless processions to abolish the Means Test, she denounced Fascist aggression in Abyssinia from innumerable platforms, and finally took off to drive an ambulance in beleaguered Madrid.

At the outbreak of war she returned to her easel but with the invasion of Russia she immediately identified herself with the Allied cause. She organized exhibitions of Soviet handicrafts, sat on committees and often, after a heavy day's work, would spend the night-hours writing 'Open a Second Front Now' on the walls of the Middlesex Hospital. After the final victory the joy she naturally experienced at the coming to power of a Labour government was soon eroded, and she was back on the barricades. It was during an Aldermaston march that she first met her husband, Dr. Wraclaw Golobcek, a Croatian economist, at that time a lecturer at L.S.E., subsequently a fellow of Balliol College, Oxford. Their marriage has always been a completely unselfish relationship, both taking an active part in the struggle against Imperialism, Neo-Colonialism and Male Chauvinism. Organizing Secretary of Peeresses for Peace, President of the Boar's Hill Branch of the International Maoist Association and an active patroness of Women's Lib, she still finds time for literature, and last year her book *The Life and Thought of John Berger* was awarded the coveted Prix Femina-Vie Malheureuse.

'URSULA'
Mark Gertler

WILLIAM succeeded his father as 8th Earl in 1937. A sunny-natured lad he was educated at Eton and Christ Church, Oxford, where he took a leading part in all the social activities of the day. Naturally a nervous speaker, the need he experienced to fortify himself before his few appearances at the Union frequently obscured the depth and originality of his political thinking, but at Bullingdon dinners he invariably proved an unqualified success. Over the sticks he displayed a skill to rival that of Lord Longford (Frank Pakenham as he then was) while his performance as Sir Andrew Aguecheek in *Twelfth Night* gained for him a reputation that extended far beyond the O.U.D.S. On going down, after his final and, alas, unsuccessful attempt to pass 'Divvers', he entered the Household Cavalry and in 1931, after several successful seasons as the principal 'deb's delight' of his day, he married. Shortly afterwards, on the occasion of his father's ninth stroke, he resigned his commission in order to give more time to helping his mother in the management of the Estate. On the outbreak of war he rejoined his regiment and served with distinction in North Africa and Italy. Early in 1945 he was 'dropped' on the headquarters of the Rumanian Resistance which existed, he was pained to discover, almost exclusively in the imagination of G.H.Q. Cairo. However, he was able, after many difficulties, to make his way to Turkey disguised as Princess Bibesco.

His Lordship's appearances in the Upper House, although infrequent, have not been ineffective and it was largely due to his efforts that the Second Reading of the Hedgehogs Protection Bill was successfully carried. Although shunning the limelight, his influence, particularly in local affairs, is great and in 1970 his tact and discretion were largely responsible for the re-routing of the M.17 through a neighbour's park some fifteen miles distant from the Abbey.

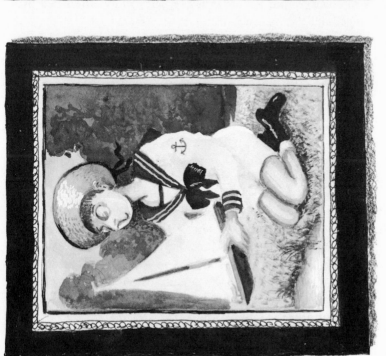

AS A CHILD   THE 8TH EARL OF LITTLEHAMPTON

WHEN VISCOUNT DRAYNEFLETE

Jacques Emile Blanche   Sir Oswald Birley, R.A.

LADY LITTLEHAMPTON is the only daughter of Sir Julian Manifest, Bt. and the Lady Claribel Manifest, third daughter of the 5th Marquess of Pontefract. Her father, who came of a long line of distinguished diplomatists, was himself the grandson of Sir Tresham Manifest and the 3rd Countess of Littlehampton and, as various portraits in the present collection so clearly show, it was from her celebrated great-grandmother that his daughter inherited her looks. Her youth was passed almost entirely in London and the English countryside as her father served his whole career in the Foreign Office and was never known to have crossed the Channel except for a single week-end at Dieppe.

Coming out at the end of the 1920s her vivacity and beauty rendered her outstanding even in a generation which included such glamorous contemporaries as Miss Nancy Mitford, Miss Maureen Guinness and Miss Rosemary Hope-Vere. After her wedding to her distant cousin, Viscount Drayneflete, which packed St. Margaret's and took up six pages of *The Tatler*, the young couple settled down in a small but beautifully decorated house in Hill Street which served as the background for many a gay party, duly chronicled by Lord Donegal and Patrick Balfour.

With the outbreak of war the new Countess (her husband had succeeded to the title on the death of his father in 1937) at once revealed her true character, which had hitherto lain largely un-detected behind what seemed, perhaps, a rather frivolous façade. At various times she worked in M.I.5., M.I.6., S.O.E., P.W.E. and the Y.W.C.A. as well as constantly liaising with the Free French. In 1943 she was attached to our Embassy in Cairo, where her lovely flat on Gezireh quickly became a home from a home for all members of White's serving in that theatre.

Since the war she has frequently thought of standing for Parlia-ment but as on some matters she is far to the right of Mr. Enoch Powell, and on others well to the left of Mr. Michael Foot, she has never yet succeeded in being adopted by any of the three major parties. However, she has done sterling work as Chairman of the Planning Committee of her local council, where she sits as an Independent, and it is largely due to her efforts that the Drayneflete Green Belt is still intact.

THE COUNTESS OF LITTLEHAMPTON

AT THE TIME OF HER COMING OUT

WHEN FULLY OUT

Sir John Lavery, R.A.

Augustus John, O.M., R.A.

FEW DÉBUTANTES of the 1950s aroused such general admiration or received so much publicity as the 8th Earl's elder daughter. Lively, energetic and scornful of convention – she was put on probation for the first time for 'pushing' cannabis at Queen Charlotte's Ball – she soon became a leading member of the so-called 'Chelsea Set'. At various times she ran a disco, a bistro and a boutique, but finally wearying of the shoddy glitter of the King's Road, after a short spell at the University of Sussex, she took up social work and moved to Peckham Rye. Here she produced her celebrated best-seller *Up the Spout*, a fearless and exhaustive study of the manners and morals of darkest Lewisham which went into three (rather small) editions and gained for her the Vanessa Redgrave Memorial Award.

In 1963 she announced her engagement to Sid Krackle, the well-known dramatist and pillar of The Royal Court, but broke it off after the birth of their first child.

Some years later she founded The Theatre of the Totally Absurd in a converted gasometer on Hackney Marshes which opened, and closed, with the celebrated production of *Where the Rainbow Ends* in the nude, with very incidental music by Stockhausen and the dialogue rewritten in very basic English. Then, in 1971, after a short period as Fashion Editor of *Private Eye* and a brief appearance in the chorus-line of *Hair* she retired to Majorca, where she is at the moment engaged on writing her autobiography.

Despite the fullness of her life and the wide range of her interests she has always remained an affectionate and dutiful daughter, and, although she is still unmarried, a devoted mother.

'JENNIFER'
John Bratby

TORQUIL, the son and heir of the present Earl, had a perfectly conventional upbringing – Eton, which he left under the usual cloud, and King's College, Cambridge, whence he was sent down in his second year for organizing a pro-Lumumba demonstration during the Annual Carol Service. Coming to London he naturally gravitated to his sister's set in the King's Road where, having always been handy with a Kodak, he set himself up as a freelance photographer. Unfortunately, being only a Viscount, and with a courtesy title at that, he soon found the competition of the Earls too great and abandoned photography for music. As he had always had a charming voice – his rendering of 'O for the Wings of a Dove' had aroused unavowable emotions in many an Etonian breast at numerous school concerts – and had also inherited much of his paternal grandmother's histrionic ability, he soon made a name for himself as a vocalist with several of the pop groups flourishing at that period. In 1969 he formed his own ensemble, the Draynes, and was soon figuring regularly in the charts. In the following year he hit the jack-pot with his highly personal version of 'Jesus Wants Me for a Sunbeam', which remained Top of the Pops for no less than thirteen weeks in succession. After an immensely successful tour of the United States he concluded a very gratifying contract with I.T.V. and now enjoys a Saturday-night 'spot' on no fewer than five stations. He has recently acquired a large mansion with two swimming-pools at St. George's Hill, Weybridge, a yacht and a villa in Barbados. He married, in 1972, Anna Maria Teresa Tombola (Miss British Honduras 1971) and they have one son, the Master of Lochwhistle. When interviewed on television about her son's achievement, Lady Littlehampton expressed great pride in his success, stressing that he was completely self-taught; his father said that he, personally, did not think he was a patch on Nellie Wallace.

VISCOUNT DRAYNEFLETE
From the sleeve of his current L.P.

U NLIKE her elder sister, the second daughter of the present Earl has always shunned the social limelight. Inheriting to the full her Great-Aunt Agatha's equestrian enthusiasm, she remained until her marriage firmly based on Drayneflete, devoting herself to pony clubs and hunter trials. Great, therefore, was the general surprise, in which it is suggested she herself shared, when her engagement was announced to a young man who was nursing the constituency as a Conservative, whom she had met quite casually at a local point-to-point.

Basil Cantilever is the only son of that distinguished architect, Sir Frederick Cantilever, O.M., R.A., P.R.I.B.A., who has made so many changes in London's skyline during the last quarter of a century. On coming down from Cambridge he entered his father's office where he was quick to concentrate on the organizational rather than the creative side of his profession. In 1963, he joined the board of Cantilever Securities which he built up into one of the largest of property companies and of which in 1967 he became Chairman. At the same time he did sterling work in local government, becoming a member both of the Westminister City Council and the G.L.C. Two years later he was returned for Drayneflete at a by-election and at the same time had the satisfaction of learning that his family firm had won the international competition for the design of a Parliamentary Sports Club and Bingo Hall which it is hoped will shortly be erected on the site of Inigo Jones's Banqueting House. A year previously he had succeeded to his father's seat on the Royal Fine Art Commission. His reputation in the House stands high and at the last Government reshuffle he was appointed P.P.S. to the Minister of Exploitation.

In his wife's family, however, it must regretfully be admitted that admiration is tempered with criticism. The present Earl's prejudice against all politicans, particularly in the Lower House, has not diminished with the years, while Lady Littlehampton's deepest feelings were outraged by the demolition of St. Ursula-inside-the-Wardrobe (with which the family had had such a long connection) acquired by her son-in-law from the Church Commissioners in 1968 for a very reasonable sum, and the erection, on the site, of Cantilever House, a thirty-storey block of offices all of which still happily remain unlet.

BASIL CANTILEVER ESQ. AND THE LADY PATRICIA CANTILEVER
David Hockney

Drayn